David Suzuki

THE TREE SUITCASE

ILLUSTRATED BY

Yvonne Cathcart

SOMERVILLE HOUSE, USA

FIRST EDITION
ISBN 1-58184-017-9
A B C D E F G H I

Designed by Gordon Robertson
Edited by Jennifer Glossop
Conifer consultant: Terence Blake
Printed in Hong Kong

Somerville House, USA is distributed by
Penguin Putnam Books for Young Readers,
345 Hudson Street, NY, 10014

Published in Canada by Somerville House Publishing
a division of Somerville House Books Limited
3080 Yonge Street, Suite 5000
Toronto, Ontario M4N 3N1

For my father. – Y.C.

The tree illustrated in this book is the Colorado blue
spruce (*Picea pungens*), sometimes known as the blue fir.

"Time to get ready to go back to the city, Peter," Grandma called across the yard.

"But I want to climb the big spruce tree again!" said Peter.

"Sorry," Grandma replied, gathering up her gardening tools. "Your mom will be here soon. But you could take the tree home."

Peter rolled his eyes. "Mom's car is bug-sized! I can barely fit my hockey stick in."

But Grandma continued. "The first thing we'll need is a suitcase."

"A suitcase, for a tree?"

Grandma laughed. "Grab that old coffee can we were using to water the garden. It will be perfect."

"It's awfully small," said Peter. "What can we pack in there?"

"See that pile of magic soil?" asked Grandma, pointing to the bottom of the garden. "Pack some of that."

5

Peter kneeled beside the full can and sifted the soil with his fingers. "Grandma, this is just dirt. Where's the magic?"

"All dirt is magical."

"Aha! Try telling that to my mom."

Grandma smiled. "Soil is magical because it is very, very old."

"As old as . . . as old as . . . Ms. Diaz, my first-grade teacher?"

"Much older. Billions of years ago, before anything lived on our planet, there was no soil. Just rocks."

"So where did the dirt come from? Alien dump-trucks from Orion?"

"Or maybe even another galaxy?" Grandma laughed. "No. That's not how it happened!"

"Long ago, earthquakes and glaciers and volcanos cracked the rocks and scattered them. Violent winds, downpours of rain, and bitter frosts helped break the rocks up, too. Then rivers and streams washed bits of rock, gravel, and sand down from the mountains and hills – right into my yard!"

Peter poked at the soil again. "This isn't just ground-up rocks. There are bits of leaf and a weird bug and – look at this – half a dead worm!"

"Right," said Grandma. "Soil contains lots of stuff – plants and insects and other animals that have died. And all kinds of worms and other small animals live in it."

"Sounds crowded!" said Peter.

"Nature doesn't waste anything," Grandma explained. "Think about the potato peelings and onion skins we put in the compost heap. When we spread the compost on the garden, those vegetables help make your tree grow big and healthy."

"Just like me. Mom says vegetables make me grow big and healthy, too. What else shall I pack for the tree, Grandma?"

"Here, take my teacup and mix about three cups of magic water from the rain barrel with the soil."

"Magic water?" Peter asked.

"Yes, it's very old water."

"No, it's not. It's from yesterday's thunderstorm."

"It fell from the clouds yesterday, but the water is even older than the soil. Water on the ground and in the seas and rivers evaporates, and then –"

"I know. Then it forms clouds. Then it rains. And then the sun comes out and the water evaporates – again – and then it forms clouds – again – and then . . ."

"Yes . . . all the way back to a time long before the dinosaurs."

"Cool! I'm drinking Brachiosaurus water."

"This water has been inside thousands of animals, Peter. And in flowers and weeds and vegetables and trees. Most of what animals have inside their skins is made up of water. Plants are mostly made of water, too."

"But how do plants drink water? They don't have mouths or tongues."

"Plants drink water through their roots. That's why we need to pack water in the tree's suitcase."

"Grandma, I think you are tricking me. All we have is a coffee can full of mud. How are Mom and I going to get that tree to the city?"

"Well, okay. You're right. That tree isn't going anywhere."

"I knew it! I just knew it! I can't even trust my own grandmother!"

Grandma tried to look hurt, but she broke out laughing. "Look under the tree, Peter. You'll find a present."

"Hooray, Christmas in July!" Peter raced across the yard to the tree.

"Are you sure, Grandma? There's only a bunch of cones."

"Right – and they're the greatest magic of all! Bring one here."

"Oh, Grandma. You think everything is magic."

"You remember the story of Jack and the Beanstalk, don't you?"

"Of course. 'Fe Fi Fo Fum, I smell the blood of an Englishman!'" Peter roared.

"This magic cone holds magic seeds. If we planted one in our magic soil, it would grow into a gigantic tree just like that one over there."

"I get it!" Peter exclaimed. "The seeds travel. The trees stay put!"

"The cones shoot their seeds from the tops of the trees – millions of seeds each year. Birds and animals and rain carry the seeds far away."

"Peter! Why are you blowing on your tree?"

"Ms. Diaz told us that plants need carbon dioxide that we breathe out. And in return, they make the oxygen that we need to live. So the tree and I are working together to make brand new air."

"Air isn't new, Peter. It's always the same oxygen and carbon dioxide."

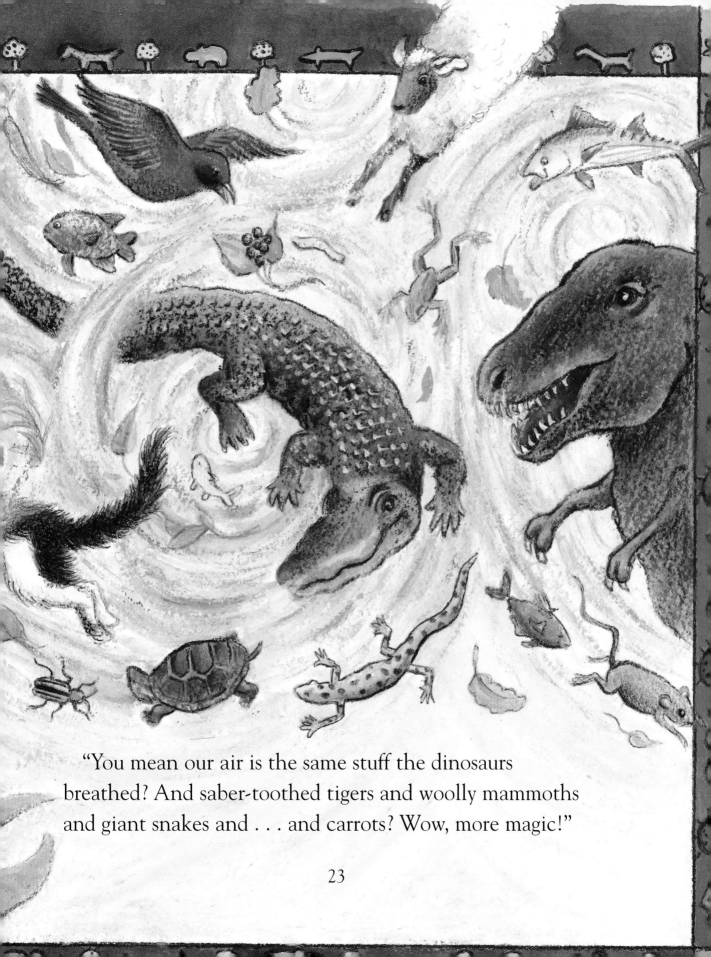

"You mean our air is the same stuff the dinosaurs breathed? And saber-toothed tigers and woolly mammoths and giant snakes and . . . and carrots? Wow, more magic!"

Peter thought for a moment. "What shall we feed my tree?"

Grandma smiled, "The magic light of the sun."

"Plants eat sunlight?"

"They catch the light in their green leaves, or needles, and change it into sugar," Grandma replied. "Plants make their own food."

"So when I eat a salad, I'm eating the sunlight caught by the plant. All right! The Mighty Cosmo-Ray Boy!"

Peter studied the little seed in his hand. "Grandma, when seeds are growing up, how do they know what they're going to be?"

"They have built-in codes."

"Codes are secret messages, aren't they?"

"Right! And the codes tell the seeds what to be when they grow up."

"So that's why those carrot seeds we planted this spring have become carrots, not watermelons!"

Peter looked puzzled. "But how will I know which way to plant the seed? I wouldn't want our tree to grow upside down."

"The magic code from that tiny seed tells the roots to dig down into the ground to anchor the new plant," explained Grandma.

"And then it will send up shoots looking for the air and light that it needs to grow big and strong," Peter exclaimed. "My tree will be huge!"

Grandma laughed. "And one day you'll grow big and tall, just like the tree."

"You have a magic code inside your own body, too," said
Grandma. "That's how it knew to make you a boy and not
a tree."

"Grandma, you are amazingly weird," said Peter, giving
her a hug. "Thanks for the tree suitcase. I'll plant the seed
as soon as I get home!"

The Tree Suitcase

Let's look again at what Peter and his grand-mother packed in the suitcase.

Soil

Soil is made up of lots of things. Tiny bits of rock that have been broken off large rocks over millions of years give the trees something solid to hold on to and provide mineral nutrients. Rotted plants and animal parts provide food, too. Soil also contains living plants and animals, some so small you need a microscope to see them.

Water

All living things need water. Water is constantly being taken out of the oceans and turned into clouds. It then returns to earth as rain and snow. This process is referred to as the hydrologic cycle.

Sunlight

Chlorophyll (which makes tree needles and leaves green) traps the energy of sunlight in a process called photosynthesis. Trees use the energy of sunlight to change carbon dioxide into sugars and starch, which provide the energy plants need to live and grow.

Seeds

Different kinds of trees have different kinds of seeds. The seeds of pines, spruces, and firs (or conifers) are found in cones. These cones protect the seeds from forest fires and pests. The cones of some conifers release their seeds slowly, over one or more years, as the cones dry out. In some pines, fire is needed to open the cones. Seed wings allow the seeds to glide far from the tree, until they fall into nooks and crannies in the soil. Many of the seeds are eaten by birds, rodents, and insects, particularly ants. The ones that are left are protected over the winter by the snow. In the spring they germinate and grow rapidly into trees.

The Magic Code

As with other living things, trees contain a magic code that tells them how to grow. This code (or DNA sequences) is found in the tree's genes, found within each cell, including seeds.

Trees are amazing!

Did you know that trees can pump water?

Hidden in the soil, roots make up to one-third of the weight of a tree. Roots help to support the tree. They also pull water from deep in the soil. This water can also help other plants. Tree roots, particularly those close to the surface, also absorb nutrients.

Did you know the difference between a conifer and a deciduous tree?

There are two kinds of trees. Conifers have needles, which they keep for many years. Deciduous trees have broad leaves, which they shed each fall. Most conifers are classified as softwoods, and deciduous trees are hardwoods. Conifers evolved more than 280 million years ago. They are very long-lived. Some giant redwoods and bristlecone pines may live for several thousand years.

Did you know that trees clean up pollution?

Trees take poisons from the soil, air, and water and trap them in their wood fibers and roots. They release friendly water and carbon dioxide back into the atmosphere.

Did you know that trees stop erosion?

Trees also help prevent erosion. Their roots anchor the soil, soak up water, and slow water run-off. Trees also help make soil. When trees blow over, their roots pull up out of the ground, breaking up the bedrock and exposing the lower soil to weathering, which releases nutrients.

Did you know we are more watery than trees?

Humans and animals are made mainly of water. Since trees are woody, they contain less water. Different types of trees contain different amounts of water, and the time of year makes a difference, too. When it is hot and dry, trees lose water. A large tree may drink hundreds of gallons of water every day.